# ASSESSING WRITING

## WRINKLES IN TEACHING:
## A SERIES OF GUIDEBOOKS FOR TEACHERS

*Wrinkle* is "a useful piece of information," and as one dictionary illustrates, "Learning the *wrinkles* from someone more experienced saves time." In the case of teaching, it also promotes faster, more effective student learning, it prevents unnecessary and frustrating bouts of trial and error, and it results in greater satisfaction with the work. The "someone more experienced" is Billie Birnie, who taught successfully in elementary, middle, and senior high schools and then went on to observe and teach hundreds of teachers and, eventually, to write about her observations and experiences. Her books, designed for both elementary and secondary teachers (and this one for school leaders and evaluators as well) are short, practical, and down-to-earth conversations about the craft of teaching. *Assessing Writing: A Guide for Teachers, School Leaders, and Evaluators* is the fourth in the series. It follows books on classroom management and differentiated instruction, organizational strategies, and parenting and learning disabilities (this one by Susan Maynard). Readers are welcome to suggest additional topics for the series. Suggestions should be sent to Rowman & Littlefield.

# ASSESSING WRITING

## A GUIDE FOR TEACHERS, SCHOOL LEADERS, AND EVALUATORS

*Billie F. Birnie*

ROWMAN & LITTLEFIELD
*Lanham • Boulder • New York • London*

Published by Rowman & Littlefield
A wholly owned subsidiary of The Rowman & Littlefield Publishing Group, Inc.
4501 Forbes Boulevard, Suite 200, Lanham, Maryland 20706
www.rowman.com

Unit A, Whitacre Mews, 26-34 Stannary Street, London SE11 4AB

British Library Cataloguing in Publication Information Available

**Library of Congress Cataloging-in-Publication Data Available**
ISBN 978-1-4758-2949-5 (pbk. : alk. paper)
ISBN 978-1-4758-2950-1 (electronic)

♾️™ The paper used in this publication meets the minimum requirements of American National Standard for Information Sciences—Permanence of Paper for Printed Library Materials, ANSI/NISO Z39.48-1992.

Printed in the United States of America

# CONTENTS

# CONTENTS

# PREFACE

This is a book I wish I had had when I started teaching. The lessons in it are hard-earned, gained from trial and error, scholarly research, help from master teachers, and, finally, years of applying and refining assessment practices that make sense.

I had the great good fortune early in my career to teach in elementary, middle, and senior high school. I taught English, journalism, and social studies. In all of those subjects, students wrote—a great deal. I was faced with hundreds of papers week after week, year after year, and since I didn't know then what I learned later, I can honestly say that I worked harder than the students.

Fortunately, I sought and found stellar mentors, and when I left the schoolhouse for a time to complete my doctorate in teaching and learning, I studied the research on assessment. My skill improved, and as it did, the writing and thinking of my students improved as well. Since then, I've been able to share with teachers, school leaders, and evaluators the practices that follow, and now I offer them to you in a single, organized collection. I hope they may save you from some of the pitfalls I encountered.

# ACKNOWLEDGMENTS

I am grateful to many friends and colleagues for their influence on my thinking and development in the field of writing assessment. Those who played the greatest roles follow:

- Colleagues in the English departments at Miami Killian and Miami Southridge Senior High School, especially Barbara Lamb, Paul Rice, Fran Ginsberg, and Mary Seamans, fellow searchers for answers to questions about evaluation;
- Professionals from the Glazer-Lorton Writing Institute, especially cofounder Eveleen Lorton and consultants Fran Claggett, Dan Kirby, Marion Davies Toth, Anna Jordan, and Helen Hollingsworth, all of whom offered practical strategies for effective assessment;
- R. Scott Baldwin, former professor at the University of Miami, who encouraged my work in the field;
- Phyllis Cohen, former deputy superintendent of the Miami-Dade County Schools, who asked me to conduct schoolwide assessments in elementary, middle, and senior high schools;
- Instructional leaders in Monroe and Palm Beach County, who asked for district-wide assessments;
- Jenny Krugman, recently retired vice president of the College Board, who brought her experience in large-scale assessment to those early projects;

## ACKNOWLEDGMENTS

- Sister Suzanne Cooke, formerly headmistress of Carrollton School of the Sacred Heart and now head of the Conference of Sacred Heart Schools, for her commitment to long-term assessment and instructional improvement; Olen Kalkus, head master of Carrollton, who continues leading the work; Lyana Azan, chair of English Language Arts, who facilitates the assessment and scoring; directors Suzanne Dempf, Lourdes Wood, Heather Gillingham-Rivas, and Paola Consuegra, who monitor test administration; and the teachers, all of whom participate every year in the studies of interrater reliability and many of whom have made valuable suggestions for improving both the process and the rubric.

I especially appreciate the help of Ms. Azan, who read the manuscript and offered constructive suggestions.

Thanks, too, to Tom Koerner, Carlie Wall, and Will True, all from Rowman & Littlefield, as well as Anita Singh of Deanta Global Publishing Services.

Finally, I wish to thank my husband Richard, who accompanies me on every step of this journey, offering encouragement, counsel, and support.

Billie Birnie
Alpine, Texas
March 10, 2016

# INTRODUCTION

If you teach a subject that requires your students to write—and most should, at least to some extent—your life as a teacher is about to get a lot easier. The practices described in this short book have the potential to transform the way you assign and assess student writing. Faithfully executed, they will yield more streamlined and focused responses from you and better thinking and writing on the part of your students. You will not only save time, you'll also increase your efficacy as a teacher.

Following the practices for individual teachers is a section on how to conduct on-demand, timed writing assessments, useful not only to teachers but also to school leaders and evaluators. Whether you want to measure the skill of students in one grade or several, one school or a whole district, the guidelines here offer step-by-step procedures for conducting larger assessments.

The book concludes with a section on developing and measuring inter-rater reliability: the extent to which assessors agree on the quality of writing. This discussion will be useful to groups of grade-level teachers, academic departments, and whole faculties. The more teachers agree on how to assess the quality of students' thinking and writing, the more consistent their expectations and grading will be. Such consistency can mightily improve the effectiveness of a school's academic program.

This book is for writers and teachers of writing—and for school leaders and evaluators who have experience as both. It focuses not on what good writing is but on the process of assessment. Those who need a refresher course on writing will be well served by reading (or rereading) Strunk and White's *Elements of Style* and Virginia Tufte's *Artful Sentences: Syntax as Style*.

# ASSESSMENT PRACTICES FOR TEACHERS

No matter what grade you teach, your primary aim in assessing writing and thinking should be to improve both. To do that, you must always focus primarily on the thinking that the writing represents and answer the question: *To what extent has the writer effectively communicated that thinking?* As you employ the strategies discussed below, use them to help answer that question.

## PRIMARY GRADES

If you teach in the primary grades, kindergarten through second, you already know that children's writing and thinking are at the emergent stage. Your charges develop at varying rates, moving from drawing to scribble writing to forming letters and, eventually, writing words and sentences. Their writing is greatly influenced by the reading, speaking, and listening they do. The richer the linguistic environment, the quicker they will progress.

By the end of second grade, the most advanced students will be writing very short "stories," and most will be able to respond to questions in writing and to write descriptive statements about pictures and other objects. Your role demands that you support each child with encouragement and guidance, offering instruction as the child becomes ready to receive it.

Assessment includes helping students develop confidence in their translation of thinking into writing (which is thinking made visible), teaching the

writing process (prewriting, drafting, revising, sharing), guiding their forma-
tion of letters and spelling, and helping them recognize and apply the five
requirements of a complete sentence:

- A capital letter at the beginning;
- A punctuation mark—period, question mark, or exclamation point—at
  the end;
- A subject—who or what the sentence is about;
- A predicate—words that tell what the subject is or does; and
- A complete thought.

## GRADES 3 THROUGH 12

The practices that follow are useful to any teacher responsible for assessing
student writing in the intermediate, middle, and high school grades:

- **Know your purpose for assessing the writing at the outset.** Are you
  judging the assignment to gauge students' understanding of a topic?
  To assign a grade? To diagnose writing skill? To determine placement in a course (such as honors, remedial, college bound, Advanced
  Placement)? To evaluate the instructional program? All of those are
  legitimate purposes for assessing student writing, and each demands a
  particular kind of assessment. The point here is that you need to know
  *before* making the assignment the purpose of the assessment.

  You also need to know whether the assessment is to be formative
  or summative. If formative, it will be designed to provide students
  with responses that will improve their learning and their writing skill;
  if summative, it will be designed to measure performance up to that
  point, such as at the end of a unit or a semester.

- **Select the type of assessment that will best achieve your purpose:
  holistic, primary trait, or analytic.**

  *Holistic assessment* considers the paper as a whole and requires
  only the assignment of an overall score (e.g., 1, 2, 3, or 4), designa-
  tion (e.g., excellent, good, fair, inadequate), or grade (e.g., A, B, C, D).

It is especially useful both for judging essays that help to place students in courses or study groups and for grading final examinations (when there will be no opportunity for students to build on a close analysis of their papers).

*Primary trait evaluation* considers only one or a very few aspects of thinking and writing; all others are excluded from the scoring. For instance, if you have been teaching the function of a topic sentence, you might well want to judge papers solely on whether the topic sentence does what it should: tell what the paragraph will be about and what the author will say about the subject. If the topic sentence introduces the subject and predicts what will be said and if the rest of the paragraph fulfills the promise, then the paper is satisfactory. If not, the paper is unsatisfactory. ("Satisfactory" and "unsatisfactory," of course, can easily be converted to grades.)

*Analytic scoring* demands that all aspects of writing be considered: the quality of thinking, the focus of the paper, the organization and development of ideas, the precision of word choice, and the use of conventions of English (e.g., usage, spelling, capitalization, punctuation, grammar). It is particularly appropriate for major assignments that require synthesis of thinking and writing skill.

Whichever type of assessment you use, be sure that its *primary* emphasis is on the quality of thinking that it represents rather than on the mechanics of writing. Maintaining that emphasis, especially when scoring analytically, can be a challenge; it's much easier to find misspelled words than to assess the quality of discourse, and those notations for mechanics sometimes tend to overshadow the more important aspects of composition.

- **Craft crystal-clear assignments.** Structure your assignment so that students know exactly what is expected of them. Give it to them in writing so they can refer to it as they work. Discuss it with them, invite questions about it, and clarify anything that might be confusing.

- **When possible, show students models or mentor texts that illustrate the assignment.** The models may come from outside sources or you may write them. They should exemplify what you expect from the students. If you give the same assignment year after year, you may have models written by former students that will serve the purpose. (For a full discussion of using models, see Birnie 2015 and Gallagher 2011.)

- **Before students write, review the purpose for assessment and the aspects of thinking and writing that will be judged.** If the purpose and scoring are to be simple, an explanation will suffice; if complex, you will want to design or select a rubric that clearly delineates the targets and shows the weight assigned to each.

- **If you want students to feed back information that you or the text (or another learning experience) has provided, use some means other than composition, such as fill in the blanks or short answer.** Compositions should be reserved for writing that demands thinking beyond recall.

- **Remember that you don't have to grade, or even read, everything that your students write.** In most academic subjects, students do a great deal of writing to learn quick writes, notes from texts and lectures, writing that clarifies their thinking or records questions about the work, journals, and so forth. The aim of that kind of writing is to facilitate student learning; it does not need to be assessed by the teacher.

- **Unless the writing is an examination or an on-demand assignment intended to gauge the skill of students at that moment, be sure that you are not the first reader of the paper.** Students can work in structured peer response groups (see Birnie 2015 for specific instructions), or they may choose peers or adults to read and respond to their papers. After receiving suggestions from those preliminary readers, students should revise and edit their papers before turning them in for formal assessment. If a rubric is being used to guide the assessment, the preliminary readers may use it to structure their responses.

- **To the extent possible, grade complete class sets of papers in one sitting without distractions or interruptions.** This one practice will save you more time and increase your effectiveness as an assessor more than any other. Used in connection with the other suggestions, it will streamline your grading. Find a quiet place, block off the time necessary to complete a set of papers (that time will obviously vary with the length and complexity of the papers), review the assignment and grading criteria, and then grade the papers.

- **Remember that you are an assessor, not an editor.** Your job is not to rewrite the paper or to carry on a written dialogue with the student. It is to assess the quality of thinking and writing. Some teachers take pride in the fact that they write more on the students' papers than the students do. Such writing, for the most part, is unproductive; it rarely produces improved writing on the part of the students.

- **Write comments that praise up to three specific strengths of the paper.** Generic praise such as "Wow!" or "Great job!" does nothing to let the student know what was done well. Such comments might be used, but if they are, they should always be accompanied by specific comments such as these:

  - "Excellent examples to support your argument."
  - "Exceptionally fine organization of the sub-topics."
  - "Strong verbs throughout."
  - "Ample variety in sentence structure."

- **Reserve suggestions for improvement for the end of the paper or a designated place on the rubric.** Keep suggestions to a minimum (no more than three is a good rule of thumb), and make suggestions that are accessible to the student—that is, suggestions that the student will understand and be able to act on. Comments such as these are appropriate:

  - "More examples would strengthen your argument."
  - "Transitional words would help the reader move more easily from one idea to the next."
  - "Check all of your pronouns to be sure they agree with antecedents in person, case, number, and gender."
  - "Find precise words to replace the slang."

- **Establish and maintain "non-negotiables."** Non-negotiables are those essential skills that all students in a class have mastered and that are therefore no longer "up for discussion." Having mastered them, students are responsible for consistently demonstrating them in their writing.

  Such non-negotiables might be writing in complete sentences, using pronouns whose antecedents are clear, spelling frequently used words correctly, or using verbs that agree with their subjects. Displaying a list of the non-negotiables in a prominent place in the classroom allows students to check their assignments against the list.

- **Select or create proofreading notations that you prefer, and use them consistently.** Give students a copy and be sure they understand what every notation means. (A suggested collection is included as appendix A.)

- **Require format that facilitates ease in scoring.** If the assignment is to be handwritten, use a guide sheet that students place beneath unlined paper or use special lined paper with wide margins. If the assignment is completed on a computer, ask students to double-space and use the fourteen-point Times Roman font.

- **Involve the students in self-assessment through the use of portfolios.** Every student should keep a portfolio of writing—drafts, completed assignments, voluntary efforts, ideas for future papers, and so forth.

  Periodically, students should be asked to evaluate some of the writing in the portfolio, either for specific, targeted skills (e.g., "Choose one completed paper from your portfolio and read it for variety in sentence length and structure. Report your findings in writing.") or for overall quality (e.g., "Choose one paper from your portfolio that pleases you; write a comment about why you like that paper and submit both the paper and the comment to your teacher.")

- **For assignments that have been scored analytically, require students to respond in writing to your assessment.** Ask them to study your notations, read your comments, and then write a brief message to you about how they will benefit from your assessment in the next assignment.

Such a message from an elementary student might be something like this: "I have to learn how to stick to the topic and not wander around so much. Also, I have to remember to use vivid verbs when they fit what I want to say."

A secondary student might write, "The development of my ideas was uneven in this paper. In the next paper I write, I'll concentrate on finding enough support for every point I want to make. Also, I'll check the subject-verb agreement in every sentence, and I'll be sure that any pronouns I use have clear antecedents."

- **Never ask your students to write anything that you haven't written yourself.** That includes timed writing assignments, the subject of the next section.

# CONDUCTING
# A WRITING
# ASSESSMENT

In these days of high-stakes testing, instructional leaders need to know long before the "big tests" are administered how their students are likely to perform. In the field of writing, a timed assessment can provide information about individual students' strengths and needs as well as identify strengths and gaps in the instructional program. Such information is invaluable for preparing for high-stakes tests—and more important than that, for enabling students to develop effective skills in thinking and writing.

Whether you are a teacher, a school leader, or an evaluator, you will find that conducting a timed writing assessment in a school (or group of schools) will be easier and more successful if you follow these steps:

- **Determine the purpose of the assessment.** It might be for any of the following reasons:

    - To diagnose students' needs
    - To gauge the effectiveness of the writing program in order to improve it
    - To serve as a "pretest" for a standardized test in writing
    - To help determine placement in classes

Whatever the specific purpose, the third standard among the National Council of Teachers of English (NCTE) Standards for the Assessment of Reading and Writing reminds planners:

*The primary purpose of assessment is to improve teaching and learning.* Assessment is used in educational settings for a variety of purposes, such as keeping track of learning, diagnosing reading and writing difficulties, determining eligibility for programs, evaluating programs, evaluating teaching, and reporting to others. Underlying all these purposes is a basic concern for improving teaching and learning.

In this first step, professionals who will use the results of the assessment need to state clearly what results they seek and how they will be used. The purpose of the assessment will drive all of the succeeding steps.

- **Decide on the population to be tested.** If the purpose is to diagnose students' writing, it may be one class, one grade level, or the whole school. If the purpose is to evaluate the instructional program, it may be students approaching the end of a segment of schooling (e.g., primary, intermediate, middle, junior high). If the purpose is to serve as a "pretest," the assessment should be administered to students who will be taking the "real test" later in the school year or in the following year. If the test is for placement, those students whose schedules will be affected by the result should take it.

- **Decide how the papers should be scored to accomplish the purpose.** For instance, if the purpose of the assessment is to diagnose students' needs, the scoring should be analytical: it should produce a blueprint of instruction for each student tested. If the test is designed to evaluate the writing program, results don't have to be reported in as much detail, but they should be refined enough that teachers can modify the instructional program to reinforce strengths and address deficiencies.

  If the test is to serve as a "pretest" for a standardized test in writing, the scoring should mimic as closely as possible the scoring to be used on the "real" test. If the results are to be used for placement, holistic scoring will probably be sufficient.

- **Design or select a rubric.** Provided on pages 12 and 13 are rubrics that have been used successfully in numerous assessments. The first is a simple four-point rubric appropriate for holistic scoring, and the second is analytic, one that allows judgment on five aspects of writing: discourse, syntax, lexicon, conventions, and handwriting.

  Note that on the second rubric, each aspect of writing is "weighted" in order to reflect the relative importance of each (e.g., the weight for discourse is 50; for handwriting, 5).

  Both of those rubrics are appropriate for use by a single scorer or by two scorers. If two scorers read the papers, their points should be averaged for a total score unless they are more than one rating apart on any of the categories. If their ratings differ more than one point, then a third reader, someone experienced in assessment, should read the paper, and that reader's assessment should determine the score.

  If you choose to design a rubric, remember to build it around an even number of ratings. That prevents assessors from "scoring to the middle," assigning a mid-point score instead of being decisive about whether the paper belongs in the upper or the lower half of ratings. Also, be sure to pilot the use of your rubric before the actual assessment to ensure that it is valid (i.e., it measures what it purports to measure) and reliable (i.e., it produces consistent results).

- **Decide how long students will have to take the assessment.** Fifty minutes is recommended: Twenty for giving instructions, distributing and collecting materials, and thirty for writing. That's sufficient time for elementary and secondary students to produce a paper long enough to evaluate but short enough to score in a reasonable time.

- **Choose a date and time for the assessment.** The date should be one that is as free as possible of other distractions, such as a major athletic event, field trip, or approaching holiday. The best time is midmorning, when students are fully awake but still alert.

| Holistic Rubric | | Assessor_____ | |
|---|---|---|---|
| **Student's Name**_____ **Grade**_____ **Date**_____ | | | |
| **Instructions:** Circle the number that corresponds to the overall quality of the paper. | | | |
| **1** | **2** | **3** | **4** |
| This paper is the work of an emergent writer, an attempt at writing that is unable to focus on a topic and organize support for it OR This paper has so many errors in syntax, word choice, and conventions that they detract significantly from the quality of the paper OR This paper does not address the assignment. | This is a paper that demonstrates developing skill. It expresses a central idea that addresses the assignment, but there may be lapses in focus, organization, development, syntax, word choice, and/or conventions that detract from its effectiveness. | This is a competent paper. It is well-focused with a clear central idea that is adequately supported. It is coherent and it has a discernible, if inconsistent, voice. Errors in word choice and conventions are not significant enough to detract from the overall quality of the paper. | This is an exemplary paper. It is thoughtful, substantive, and focused, expressed in a consistent, engaging voice. It has a clear central idea that is logically and fully developed. Errors in word choice and conventions are not significant enough to detract from the overall quality of the paper. |

| Analytic Rubric | | | Assessor_____ | | |
|---|---|---|---|---|---|
| **Author**_____ **Grade**_____ **Topic**_____ | | | | | |
| **Instructions:** Circle the number (4, 3, 2, or 1) that corresponds to the quality of each aspect of writing. Multiply that number by the weight to arrive at points for each category. Add the points and divide by 100 to arrive at the score. | | | | | |
| **Aspect of Writing** | **Exemplary** | **Competent** | **Developing** | **Emergent** | **Weight & Points** |
| **Discourse** (a connected series of utterances; a text; thus, aspects of discourse pertain to the whole piece of writing) | 4 - An exemplary paper: thoughtful, substantive, and focused, expressed in a consistent, engaging voice; has a clear central idea that is logically and fully developed. | 3 - This is a competent paper. It is well-focused with a clear central idea that is adequately supported. It is coherent and it has a discernible, if inconsistent, voice. | 2 - This is a paper that demonstrates developing skill. It expresses a central idea that addresses the assignment, but there may be lapses in focus, organization, and/or development that detract from its effectiveness. | 1 - This paper is the work of an emergent writer, an attempt at writing that is unable to focus on a topic and organize support for it OR This paper does not address the assignment. | X 50 = _____ |
| **Syntax** (the arrangement of words and phrases to create sentences) | 4 - It is written in complete, well-formed sentences that vary in length and complexity. | 3 - With few exceptions, sentences are complete, well-formed, and varied in length and complexity. | 2 - Most sentences are complete, but they may lack variety in length and/or complexity, or some may be ill-formed. | 1 - It demonstrates little "sentence sense," with many fragments or run-ons and/or little variety in length and complexity | X 20 = _____ |

| Lexicon (vocabulary) | 4 - It employs a felicitous range of vocabulary, with no ill-chosen words and no slang or redundancy except when clearly used for effect. | 3 - It employs an appropriate range of vocabulary. | 2 - The range of vocabulary is limited and/or word choice is sometimes inadequate. | 1 - The range of vocabulary is extremely narrow. | X 15 = _____ |
|---|---|---|---|---|---|
| Conventions (the usual ways of doing something, in this case, writing English) | 4 - It adheres to Standard American English conventions of grammar, usage, spelling, punctuation, and capitalization. | 3 - With few exceptions, it adheres to Standard American English conventions. | 2 - With several lapses, it attempts to use the conventions of Standard American English. | 1 - Errors in grammar, usage, spelling, punctuation, and/or capitalization abound. | X 10 = _____ |
| Handwriting | 4 - It is neatly written in cursive handwriting. | 3 - It is legibly written in cursive handwriting. | 2 - It is legibly **printed**. | 1 - It is difficult to read. | X 5 = |
| | | | | Total Points/Score | |

- **Design or select a prompt.** Whether you design the prompt or select one from another source, it should adhere to these criteria:

  - The topic of the prompt must be accessible to all of the students who will take the test; the assessment is intended to measure thinking and writing skill, not content knowledge.
  - The topic must be broad enough that students can draw from their individual banks of knowledge to support their positions. It should elicit ideas gleaned from the students' own experience and reading, not from information memorized about a subject.
  - The topic must be significant enough to evoke thoughtful, interesting essays worthy of students' best efforts.
  - The topic must not be controversial. A controversial topic risks reader bias on the part of the assessor(s).
  - The prompt should be brief and simply stated. It should (1) introduce the topic, (2) provide some elaboration, and (3) give explicit instructions for the essay.
  - The topic may be either personal or objective. Personal prompts often produce students' best writing because of the authors'

investment in the subject. Objective topics require that students get "outside of themselves" to deal with the topic itself rather than their preferences, feelings, and attitudes. School leaders' philosophy should inform the decision about which type to use.

Here are two prompts that have been used successfully. The first, with a personal topic, was used with elementary students; the second, with an objective topic, was used with secondary students:

- Everyone does something well. One person might be good at making friends. Another might be able to cook well. Someone else may be a good reader. Other people swim, write, or play games well. Think about all of the things you have learned to do well. Choose *one* of those things and tell your reader about it.

- The theme, or main idea, of a novel is conveyed through the action of the story. Select key incidents from a novel you have read and explain how they express the theme.

○ If possible, the prompt should be held in confidence until the day of the assessment.

Additional prompts that have been used successfully in timed writing assessments are included as appendix B.

- **Prepare materials for the assessment.** Each student should receive a sheet of paper that includes these instructions: "You will have thirty minutes to write in response to the assignment below. When your teacher tells you to begin, take a few minutes to plan your paper and then begin writing. If you finish before your teacher tells you to stop, look over your paper to see if there are ways you can make it better. Make any changes you want to make and then turn in your paper when the teacher tells you to."

  Add next: "The rest of this page is yours to plan what you will write. Use it any way you wish, to scribble, cluster, draw, list, or outline your thoughts before you begin your response."

  Follow those instructions with the prompt. (See appendix C for a sample format.)

In addition to the prompt, each student should receive paper for writing the essay. Elementary school children will need no more than two pages and secondary students usually no more than four, although additional pages should be made available at both levels in case students need them. A perfect "booklet" can be constructed for secondary students by using 11" × 17" paper and folding it in half, making four pages.

The first page of each answer sheet should have space for the student's name, grade in school, and, if you like, the teacher's name. Placing that information in the upper right-hand corner facilitates processing the papers. (See appendix D for sample pages.)

- **Give instructions to teachers who will administer the test.** The following are recommended for assessments that diagnose student writing and evaluate instructional programs:

  ○ Tell your students that they will be participating in a writing assessment to measure their ability to *think and write*. They will be given an assignment, and they'll have thirty minutes to write about the topic. The topic will be one with which they are familiar. The papers will not be graded, but they will be scored, and the results will be used to judge what they know about writing and what they still need to learn. The papers will be judged on these five aspects of writing:

    - Overall thinking and organization (most important);
    - Sentence sense (completeness, correctness, and variety);
    - Word choice;
    - Mechanics (punctuation, spelling, capitalization); and
    - Handwriting (cursive is preferred).

  ○ Be sure everyone has a pen or pencil.
  ○ Distribute the answer sheets and assignments.
  ○ Tell students:

    - To write their name, grade, and teacher's name in the spaces provided.
    - When you begin timing, you will periodically alert them to the time remaining.

- If they should finish early, they should sit quietly.
- That you have extra answer sheets in case they need more space for their response.
- To follow along as you read the instructions aloud.

○ Write on the board: "Thirty minutes remaining."
○ Monitor the work by watching the students and encouraging them if necessary, but do not help them. Fifteen minutes after they start, change the sign on the board and announce fifteen minutes remaining. Post and announce the time again when there are ten minutes remaining. When five minutes remain, change the posting again and remind students that they must finish their papers in five more minutes.
○ At the end of thirty minutes, tell students to stop if they have not already finished. Ask them to put the assignments and additional pages, if they used any, with the answer sheet. Collect the papers. Give both the assignments and the essays to the person designated to collect them.

- **If either the prompt or the rubric has not been field-tested, conduct a pilot assessment.** This is a critical step if you are using untried materials. The pilot study can be much smaller in scope than the actual assessment, but you must know that the prompt will elicit students' best efforts and that the rubric will yield the most effective evaluation.

  Whether the pilot assessment is administered to a sample of students in the same school(s) where the actual assessment will take place or to students in another school, the sample should be as similar as possible to the population to be tested.

- **If the teachers whose students will be participating in the assessment have not already done so, they should experience a timed writing assignment.** Such an assignment can easily be administered in a faculty meeting, and it offers teachers the opportunity to think and write under the same kind of pressure that their students will experience. The teachers' papers do not have to be judged. Teachers should have the opportunity to talk about the experience with their colleagues, and those who wish to share their papers could do so.

This prompt has been used successfully in faculty meetings: "Think of all of the books you have read. Choose one that made a lasting impression on you. Tell your reader about how the book affected you and why you will remember it."

- **Administer the assessment.** To the extent possible, arrange for the time to be uninterrupted by public address announcements or other distractions.

- **Prepare papers for scoring.** After the papers have been collected, separate the student essays from the prompts. Then "blind" the papers by putting post-its over the students' and teachers' names. *This is an important step, as it helps to prevent reader bias.*

  Next, shuffle the papers so that they are in random order. If several classes of students in the same grade have taken the assessment, shuffle all of their papers together so that they are not identifiable as classes. Make one stack of the shuffled papers.

- **Score the papers.** Whether your score holistically or analytically, remember that in a timed assessment, students are able to produce only draft writing; they don't have time or resources to confer with peers, edit, or revise their work. Also, they are addressing an assignment they haven't seen before, and they are working under the pressure of time. Your standards therefore may be more forgiving than they would be for other writing tasks.

  If you are scoring holistically, review the descriptions of the four ratings in the rubric. Then read the first paper in the stack. (It may help to read the paper aloud.) Decide which of the four descriptions best describes it. Put it in a place on the table in front of you designated for that rating. (To be consistent with the ratings on the rubric, make the place for papers rated 1 to the far left, 2 left center, 3 right center, and 4 far right.)

  Read without a pen or pencil in your hand. Do not make any notations on the paper. (This process is the most difficult part of holistic scoring for some teachers.) Read each paper in turn, refresh your memory of the descriptions on the rubric as necessary, and sort the papers into the four stacks, one for each rating.

Don't agonize over what rating each paper deserves. Read and sort; read and sort, until you have read all of the papers.

After the first reading, you will have four stacks of papers in front of you, one for each of the ratings. At this point, you are able to confirm or change your judgment. Begin with the papers rated 4. Read each paper in the stack and decide whether it deserves the highest rating; if not, put it in the stack rated 3.

Next, read the papers in the "3 stack." If any of them should be moved to the "2 stack" or the "4 stack," put them in the appropriate place.

Continue with the papers in the "2 stack," and then finish the second reading with the papers in the "1 stack."

When you are satisfied that the papers are sorted appropriately, score them either by writing the ratings directly on the papers or by circling the rating on individual rubrics and attaching them to the papers.

If you are scoring analytically, work with the papers and rubrics one at a time. Take the first paper from the stack and have a rubric at hand. Review the descriptions of ratings for discourse. Then read the paper through without making any notations, paying attention only to elements of discourse: focus, organization, development, and voice. (It may help to read the paper aloud.) Circle the rating that best describes the discourse.

If you are new to this kind of assessment, you may want to use the "read and sort" technique described for holistic scoring to satisfy yourself on the appropriate ratings for discourse before moving on to subsequent steps in scoring.

Glance next at the handwriting; circle the rating that best describes it.

Now, with pencil in hand, read the paper again, making notations in either the left- or the right-hand margin (not in the text) about sentence structure, vocabulary, and conventions. Use the notations from appendix A or others of your choice, but be consistent.

Review the descriptions of ratings for syntax. Scan the paper for notations about sentence structure. Decide which description best fits the paper, and circle the number of that rating.

Review the descriptions of ratings for lexicon. Scan the paper for notations about vocabulary. Decide which description best fits the paper, and circle the number of that rating.

Review the descriptions of ratings for conventions. Scan the paper for notations about mechanics. Decide which description best fits the paper, and circle the number of that rating.

Remove the post-it covering the students' name and fill in the information at the top of the rubric. Multiply the ratings by the weight in the right-hand column and fill in the points. (For instance, if the rating for discourse was 3, multiply 3 by fifty for 150 points.)

Then add the points together for a score. For convenience in analysis and reporting, divide the score by 100 to arrive at score on a scale of 0 to 4.

- **Report results.** The extent to which you report results of the assessment depends on its purpose and the audience—who needs to know? If you have conducted the assessment with your own students, recording the results on a table similar to the one in appendix E will probably suffice; that will give you the information you need to reinforce strengths and to address weaknesses in the students' skills.

  On the other hand, if the assessment was designed to evaluate a school's instructional program, you will want to prepare a formal report to the faculty that includes the following:

  ○ An introduction that includes:

    - The purpose of the assessment
    - The population
    - The date
    - The method of scoring

  ○ A body that includes, for each grade tested:

    - Details about the population in that grade (number per class, teachers' names, etc.)
    - The prompt

---

- A general description about the students' response to the prompt
- A table that shows the range (lowest and highest scores), mean (average), median (the point at which half of the population scored higher and half lower), and mode (the most frequently earned score)
- Discussion of the table's contents
- If you scored analytically, a table that shows the percent of ratings (1, 2, 3, 4) in each category (discourse, syntax, lexicon, conventions, handwriting)
- Optional but highly desirable if the readers of the report are not going to see all of the papers: Sample papers that illustrate the range of writing skill in that grade. (To protect students' privacy, those papers should not include the names of students, nor should they contain content that identifies the authors. If names of students are to be used, permission must be secured beforehand from parents.)

○ If the assessment included students from more than one grade, include a section that compares performance in all grades.
○ If this assessment is one in a series such as annual assessments, include a section that compares this performance to that on earlier tests.
○ A conclusion that offers a broad analysis of performance on the assessment and recommendations for the instructional program.

The report should be disseminated to everyone who has a stake in the program, and it should be discussed thoroughly, especially with teachers whose work might be influenced by its implications and recommendations. Following are some questions to facilitate the discussion:

○ What strengths in our instructional program does the report name or imply?
○ Are the strengths at a satisfactory level or do they need to be shored up even further?

- What challenges does the report indicate?
- What specific practices will promote growth in the areas where it is most needed?
- Should those practices be implemented only in certain disciplines or across the curriculum?
- What needs to be communicated to teachers in grades other than the one(s) tested? (For instance, if the assessment tested the writing of third graders, what do the teachers in grades one and two need to know about the results? If the assessment tested the writing of tenth graders, what do teachers of grades eleven and twelve need to know about particular emphases in the instructional program being made as a result of the assessment?)
- What are our next steps?

The author of the report should be available to answer any questions that might arise.

If analytic scoring was used, all of the teachers whose students participated should complete the table of performance (appendix E) for their own students in order to tailor instruction to students' needs. If several teachers in a grade level participated, the tables will offer them useful data for grouping students for specific lessons, both within and across classes. (For instance, teachers might want to make a cross-class group of all students who had difficulty with subject-verb agreement and let that group participate in a series of lessons that cover the topic.)

Remember that the results of a writing assessment (or any evaluation, for that matter) are valuable only to the extent that they are used. Patton's *Utilization-Focused Evaluation* (1997) promotes evaluations that are conducted for and with "specific, intended primary users for specific, intended uses." If you are an external evaluator, you will also want to be sure that the assessment adheres to the American Education Association's *Guiding Principles for Evaluators.*

# ESTABLISHING INTERRATER RELIABILITY

Interrater reliability is the extent to which two or more assessors agree on the scoring of a paper. Reliability is reported either by a measure of correlation, with 1.0 being perfect, or by percent of agreement, with 100 percent being perfect. Thus, a correlation of 0.5 would indicate that assessors agreed on 50 percent of the scoring decisions.

A reasonable goal to aim for in writing assessments of K–12 student work is 75 percent reliability, as there are numerous instances in student writing that allow for reasonable differences between assessors. And to arrive at that goal, scoring needs to be more precise than has thus far been discussed.

## THE RUBRIC

One means of gaining such precision is to quantify decision points on the rubric to the extent possible. That has been done for the analytic rubric in the previous section. For studies of interrater reliability, that rubric looks like the rubric on pages 24 and 25 (see appendix F for landscape form).

Analytic Rubric, Quantified          Assessor_____

_____ No. Lines ÷ 10 = _____ (Divisor)

Author_____ Grade_____ Topic_____

| Aspect of Writing | Exemplary | Competent | Developing | Emergent | Weight & Points |
|---|---|---|---|---|---|
| **Discourse** (a connected series of utterances; a text; thus, aspects of discourse pertain to the whole piece of writing)<br><br>**Read descriptors and apply your judgment.** | 4 - An exemplary paper: thoughtful, substantive, and focused, expressed in a consistent, engaging voice; has a clear central idea that is logically and fully developed. | 3 - This is a competent paper. It is well-focused with a clear central idea that is adequately supported. It is coherent and it has a discernible, if inconsistent, voice. | 2 - This is a paper that demonstrates developing skill. It expresses a central idea that addresses the assignment, but there may be lapses in focus, organization, and/or development that detract from its effectiveness. | 1 - This paper is the work of an emergent writer, an attempt at writing that is unable to focus on a topic and organize support for it OR. This paper does not address the assignment. | X 50 = _____ |
| **Syntax** (the arrangement of words and phrases to create sentences)<br>_____ Structure (*str.*)<br>_____ Fragment (*frag.*)<br>_____ Run-on (*RO*)<br><br>☐ ÷ ___ = _____<br>(Total) (Divisor) (No. per 10 lines)<br>OR **Underline words to indicate that judgment overrides notation.** | 4 - It is written in complete, well-formed sentences that vary in length and complexity. (It has no str. & no fragments or run-ons except those used for effect.) | 3 - With few exceptions, sentences are complete, well-formed, and varied in length and complexity. (No more than 1 Str., RO, or Frag. per 10 lines) | 2 - Most sentences are complete, but they may lack variety in length and/or complexity, or some may be ill-formed. (More than 1 but fewer than 3 Str., RO, or Frag. per 10 lines) | 1 - It demonstrates little "sentence sense," with many fragments or run-ons and/or little variety in length and complexity. (3 or more Str., RO, or Frag. per 10 lines) | X 20 = _____ |

| Lexicon (vocabulary) ____ Word Choice *(wc)* [□] ÷ ____ = ____ (Total) (Divisor) (No. per 10 lines) Excessive Slang? Yes No Gross Redundancy? Yes No OR **Underline words to indicate that judgment overrides notation.** | 4 - It employs a felicitous range of vocabulary, with no ill-chosen words and no slang or redundancy except when clearly used for effect. (No *wc*, *Sl*, or *Re*) | 3 -It employs an appropriate range of vocabulary. (No more than 1 *wc* per 10 lines, no excessive slang or gross redundancy) | 2 - The range of vocabulary is limited and/or word choice is sometimes inadequate. (More than 1 but fewer than 3 *wc* per 10 lines and/or excessive slang or gross redundancy) | 1 - The range of vocabulary is extremely narrow. (3 or more *wc* per 10 lines and/or excessive slang or gross redundancy) | X 15 = ____ |
|---|---|---|---|---|---|
| **Conventions** (the usual ways of doing something, in this case, writing English) ____ Spelling ____ Subj.-Verb ____ Pronoun ____ Capitalization ____ Punctuation ____ Usage [□] ÷ ____ = ____ (Total) (Divisor) (No. per 10 lines) **No override** | 4 - It adheres to Standard American English conventions of grammar, usage, spelling, punctuation, and capitalization. (No √s) | 3 - With few exceptions, it adheres to Standard American English . conventions. (No more than 2 √s per 10 lines) | 2 - With several lapses, it attempts to use the conventions of Standard American English. (More than 2 but fewer than 7 √s per 10 lines) | 1 - Errors in grammar, usage, spelling, punctuation, and/or capitalization abound. (7 or more √s per 10 lines) | X 10 = ____ |
| **Handwriting** | 4 – It is neatly written in cursive handwriting. | 3 - It is legibly written in cursive handwriting. | 2 - It is legibly **printed.** | 1 - It is difficult to read. | X 5 = ____ |
| | | | | **Total Points/Score** | |

## PROCEDURES FOR SCORING

The procedures for scoring with this rubric differ considerably from those described in the previous section. (They are also included in appendix F so that they can be printed on the back of the landscape rubric.)

1. Review the descriptions of the ratings for discourse on the rubric.
2. Read the paper through for the quality of discourse. Try to ignore other aspects of writing. (It may help to read the paper aloud.)
3. On the rubric, circle the number of the rating for discourse.
4. Glance again at the handwriting. Circle the number of the rating. (If any of the letters are connected, the writing is considered to be cursive.)
5. On the rubric, fill in the author's name, grade in school, topic, and your name (assessor).
6. Count the number of lines in the essay, only lines that have half or more filled with writing. If the paper has a title, count it as a line. Write the number of lines in the blank provided (just below the title of the rubric). Divide by ten. Round to the nearest whole number. Write that number in the blanks labeled *divisor* in the first column after syntax, lexicon, and conventions.
7. Read the essay again, making these notations in the margin as you read:

| | |
|---|---|
| *str* | to indicate awkward or incorrect structure of a sentence |
| *frag* | to denote a fragment |
| *RO* | to denote a run-on |

NOTE: If you mark *str., frag,* or *RO*, do not mark internal errors.

| | |
|---|---|
| *wc* | to indicate inappropriate or incorrect word choice |
| *Sl* | to denote *excessive* slang (Make only once for the whole paper.) |
| *Re* | to denote *gross* redundancy (Make only once for the whole paper.) |
| *Sp* | Misspelled word |
| *S-V* | Disagreement between subject and verb |
| *Pron* | Pronoun problem |
| Cap | Capitalization error |
| Punc | Incorrect punctuation |
| Use | Any error in usage not covered by other notations |

8. Count the instances of each notation except for slang and redundancy. Write the number in the space provided on the rubric. Denote excessive slang or gross redundancy by circling *Yes* to indicate that it appeared in the essay.

9. Add the number of notations for syntax, lexicon, and conventions, recording the sums in the boxes provided.

10. For syntax, divide the total number of notations by the divisor. Apply your judgment; if your judgment overrides the numbers, underline words in the rubric that conform to your judgment. If not, use the guidelines in parentheses on the rubric to arrive at a rating. Circle the number of the rating.

11. For lexicon, divide the number of notations for word choice by the divisor. Apply your judgment; if your judgment overrides the numbers, underline words in the rubric that conform to your judgment. If not, use the guidelines in parentheses on the rubric to arrive at a rating. Circle the number of the rating.

12. For conventions, divide the number of errors by the divisor. Use the guidelines in parentheses on the rubric to arrive at a rating. Circle the number of the rating. (Note that there is no provision for override for the rating of conventions.)

13. Multiply each rating by the weight designated on the rubric, and write the number of points in the spaces provided.

14. Add the points for a total; divide by 100 to arrive at the score.

## CONDUCTING A STUDY

To conduct a study of interrater reliability with a single school's faculty (or portion thereof), select several student papers (six is a good number) that represent the range of writing skill in the whole group. "Blind" the papers by covering students' names. Assign a number to each paper. Number the lines in each paper. (The numbering facilitates discussion of the papers after the scoring.) Duplicate the papers so that every teacher participating in the study will have a complete set.

Review your own scoring of the papers. If you wish to involve other assessors whose judgment is sound, ask them to score the papers, too, and then decide on the ratings and scores that will serve as the criteria. This is an especially important step if you are working with a group of teachers who lack confidence in your judgment as an assessor. This is the point at which the criteria are negotiated. Bringing together a few teachers respected by their colleagues for this process will strengthen teachers' confidence in the criteria (and therefore in the whole process).

If you must use your own scoring as the criteria, be sure the teachers know of your experience and competence in the assessment of writing skill.

Convene the teachers who will participate in the study. Explain the value of reaching agreement on assessing students' writing and thinking. If teachers can consistently assess students' thinking and writing, they can greatly facilitate improvement in both. The more improvement, the more students will be successful, not only in the academic world, but in the larger world where their success will depend to a great extent on their ability to think critically and write effectively.

Explain what interrater reliability is, how it is calculated, and what designated ranges of reliability represent. For the purposes of this kind of study, reliability from 0 to 0.24 is considered negligible; 0.25 to 0.49 is minimal; 0.50 to 0.74 is substantial; and 0.75 to 1.0 is excellent. The goal is to achieve 0.75 or higher.

Agreement on the first four categories (discourse, syntax, lexicon, and conventions) will be considered as the same rating from the criteria and the individual assessor. Agreement on handwriting is broader: the ratings of 3 (legible cursive) and 4 (neat cursive) will be considered to be in agreement—that is, they will be considered as the same rating for the purpose of the study. (This provision is made to accommodate differences in what some people judge as *legible* and others judge as *neat*. It allows assessors to focus on the far more important aspects of thinking and writing represented by the first four categories.)

Distribute the student papers, rubrics (one per paper), and procedures (one copy per teacher, unless they are printed on the back of the rubric).

Lead the group through the scoring of one paper, following the procedures exactly as they are written and talking through all of the reasoning and notations that established the criteria for that paper. Answer any questions that arise during the process.

Ask the teachers to score the second paper on their own, following the same procedures. Encourage them to talk to one another as they work. When everyone has finished, talk through the scoring of the second paper and ask teachers to note any differences between the criteria and their own decisions. Discuss those differences and answer questions about the process.

Repeat the procedure for the third paper.

Teachers then score the remaining three papers on their own, talking with colleagues as they choose. Remind them that this is not a contest; it is an effort to reach agreement on the scoring. Conversation with colleagues helps. However, after the conversation, teachers need to make their own decisions about ratings.

Collect the scored papers and rubrics from the teachers and process them as follows:

- Check every rubric to be sure that notations and ratings agree *or* that words in the rubric are underlined to designate override of notations. Make necessary changes. If a rating is changed, write or stamp on the rubric: "Rating(s) changed to agree with notations."
- Check every rubric to be sure the score is correctly computed. Make corrections as necessary. If a score is changed, write or stamp on the rubric: "Score changed to agree with ratings."
- Keep scored papers and rubrics alphabetized by teachers' last names.

Make individual reports. Begin by creating a database that shows the ratings and scores of the criteria and the assessor, as follows. (Gray indicates agreement between the criteria and the assessor. Notice in the case of writing on Essay No. 63, the 3 and 4 are considered to be in agreement.)

| Janet Smith (a pseudonym) | | | | | | | |
|---|---|---|---|---|---|---|---|
| No. | Discourse | Syntax | Lexicon | Conventions | Writing | Score | Scorer |
| 51 | 4 | 3 | 3 | 3 | 4 | 3.55 | Criteria |
| 51 | 4 | 3 | 3 | 3 | 4 | 3.55 | Janet |
| 63 | 3 | 3 | 2 | 3 | 4 | 2.90 | Criteria |
| 63 | 3 | 2 | 3 | 2 | 3 | 2.70 | Janet |
| 75 | 2 | 2 | 2 | 3 | 4 | 2.20 | Criteria |
| 75 | 2 | 2 | 3 | 3 | 1 | 2.20 | Janet |

Continue by creating a table that shows a comparison of each teacher's ratings to the criteria as well as the percent of agreement on each category.

Write a report that explains the database and the table. (A sample report is included as appendix I.)

| Aspect of Writing | Janet's Ratings in Comparison to Criteria | | | | | |
|---|---|---|---|---|---|---|
| | Same | | Higher | | Lower | |
| | No. | % | No. | % | No. | % |
| Discourse | 3/3 | 100 | 0 | 0 | 0 | 0 |
| Syntax | 2/3 | 67 | 0 | 0 | 1/3 | 33 |
| Lexicon | 1/3 | 33 | 2/3 | 67 | 0 | 0 |
| Conventions | 2/3 | 67 | 0 | 0 | 1/3 | 33 |
| Handwriting | 2/3 | 67 | 0 | 0 | 1/3 | 0 |
| Total | 10/15 | 67 | 2/15 | 13 | 3/15 | 20 |

When all of the reports have been written, print them and organize them by teachers' last names. Proof them carefully, referring to the rubrics as the source. Correct them as necessary. Print them. Continue to keep them organized by teachers' last names.

Using the individual reports as the source, create a database (Excel is recommended software) that includes the following headings: assessor's name; any important identifying information, such as school name or grade level; reliability columns for overall, discourse, syntax, lexicon, handwriting; number of ratings same as criteria, number of ratings higher than criteria, number of ratings lower than criteria, and essays that had perfect correlation.

For the reliability entries, use percent instead of decimals (e.g., 60 instead of 0.6). In the last column, enter both the number of essays that had perfect correlation (1, 2, or 3) and the identifying number(s) assigned to the essays (e.g., from this example, number 51, 63, or 75).

Print the database and then proof it, using the individual reports as the source. Make corrections as necessary. Print the corrected version.

Attach individual reports to sets of scored papers. Keep them until the whole report is finished.

Using the large database, calculate or identify:

- Number and percent of ratings that are the same, higher, and lower than standards. (To calculate the total number of ratings, add the number of ratings for all assessors that were the same, higher, and lower. Check your answer by multiplying the number of participating teachers by fifteen, which is the number of decisions each teacher made in scoring the three papers. Calculate the percent of each by dividing the sum by the total number of ratings.) *The percent of ratings that were the same is the measure of overall interrater reliability, an important number for a faculty group to know.*

- Number and percent of assessors who attained excellent (75 to 100 percent), substantial (50 to 74 percent), minimal (25 to 49 percent), or negligible (0 to 14 percent) overall reliability.
- Number and percent of assessors who attained excellent reliability (75 percent or higher) in each category (discourse, syntax, lexicon, conventions, and handwriting).
- Names of assessors who attained perfect correlation on individual essays and identification of the essays. (If no one attained perfect correlation on an essay, you will want to examine the scoring for that one more closely to find where the disagreement lay.)
- Names of assessors who attained perfect correlation on discourse (the most important category).

Appendix H shows a sample database with preliminary calculations.

Write a report that analyzes the data. If this is one of a series of studies, make comparisons to earlier studies. For school leaders, add databases from individual reports as an appendix. Proof the report, using the database and preliminary analyses as sources.

Leave the report for a few days. (This is an important step; you will have been immersed in the data, and you will need to see it with new perspective.)

Reread the report. Revise it as necessary. When you are satisfied that it is as effective as possible, prepare it for dissemination.

Return the scored papers, rubrics, and individual reports to the teachers who participated in the study.

Provide copies of the overall report, without the individual databases, to the teachers. Provide copies with the databases to school leaders.

Meet with school leaders and teachers to discuss the report. These questions may guide the discussion:

- How close is our overall reliability (as a group) to the goal of 75 percent?
- How many of the group achieved that goal individually?
- In what categories did we most frequently agree?

- In what categories did we find the least agreement? How can we account for the lack of agreement in those categories?
- Which of the essays challenged us the most? How do we account for the challenge?
- What can we do to improve our interrater reliability in the next study?
- What are our immediate next steps?

Remember that improving interrater reliability requires five actions: creating a sound rating scale and careful definitions of criteria in the rubric, conducting a pilot study, training raters in the use of the rubric, ensuring that raters practice using the rubric, and monitoring reliability.

# APPENDIX A

# PROOFREADING

# NOTATIONS

| Notation | What It Represents |
|---|---|
| | Regarding Syntax |
| Str | Awkwardly structured sentence |
| Frag | Fragment (a group of words that does not make a complete thought) |
| RO | Run-on (two or more sentences punctuated incorrectly as one sentence |
| | Regarding Lexicon |
| wc | Word choice; an inappropriate or ill-chosen word |
| Sl | Excessive slang (mark only once for entire paper) |
| Re | Gross redundancy (mark only once for entire paper) |
| | Regarding Conventions |
| sp | Misspelled word |
| s-v | Disagreement between subject and verb |
| pron | Pronoun problem; could be an ambiguous pronoun with no clear antecedent; disagreement between pronoun and antecedent in person, case, number, or gender; incorrect use of pronoun (e.g., *who* instead of *whom*) |
| cap | Capitalization: either a word is capitalized that shouldn't be or it is not capitalized and should be |
| punc | Incorrect punctuation |
| use | Any error in usage not covered by the other notations |

# APPENDIX B
# PROMPTS APPROPRIATE
# FOR WRITING
# ASSESSMENT

All of the prompts that follow have been used successfully in timed, on-demand writing assessments. They are grouped for convenience, the first group being those that have been used with elementary (and some with secondary) students and the second being those that have been used with secondary students only.

## FOR ELEMENTARY OR SECONDARY STUDENTS

- Everyone does something well. One person might be good at making friends. Another might be able to cook well. Someone else may be a good reader. Other people swim, write, or play games well. Think about all of the things you have learned to do well. Choose *one* of those things and tell your reader about it.
- Think about all of the stories and books you have read. Choose *one* story or book that you really like and write to explain why it is special to you.
- Think about all of the things you like to do. Choose *one* of those things and tell your reader about it.
- From the time you enter kindergarten until you finish school, one of your most important responsibilities is to be a successful student. What

does it take to be a good student? What habits, skills, and attitudes contribute to success? Describe what it takes to be a successful student.

- Think about some changes that would make school better for you. Choose *one*. Tell your reader what one thing you would change and why.
- We learn many important things in school. Think about *one* thing you learned in school this year and explain to your reader why you think it is important.
- All of us have special friends. They may be classmates, neighbors, brothers, sisters, cousins, or even parents. Choose *one* of your friends. Tell your reader why that person is special to you.
- Think about all of the teachers you have had. Choose *one* that stands out for you, and write to tell your reader why that teacher is special.
- Think about all of the special places that you like to be. Choose *one* of those places and tell your reader why you like to be there.
- Good and evil are often revealed through characters in fairy tales, myths, short stories, novels, and movies. Choose *one character* from your reading or viewing and show how he or she reflects good *or* evil (not both).
- History tells us about all kinds of leaders. Choose *one leader* and tell about his or her leadership.
- Your school days include the study of many subjects: reading, writing, mathematics, history, art, computers, physical education, language, and others. Choose *one subject* and tell why it is important to learn it.
- Playing a team sport, completing a group project for school, performing in a concert or a play are just some examples of activities in which teamwork is necessary. Tell what it takes to work well with others.
- A successful person usually practices good habits of organization. What does it mean to be well organized?

## FOR SECONDARY STUDENTS

- Albert Schweitzer said, "At times our own light goes out and is rekindled by a spark from another person. Each of us has cause to think with deep gratitude of those who have lighted the flame within us." Think of the people in your life who have "lighted your flame." Choose *one of them* and tell how that person inspired you.

- Think of all of the books you have read. Choose *one* that made a lasting impression on you. Tell your reader about how the book affected you and why you will remember it.
- Sometimes, an event in history—a land discovered, a leader born, a war won or last, a medical breakthrough—has had a significant impact on the people whose lives it touched. Choose *one event* in history and tell how it affected people's lives.
- Inventions—from the wheel to the printing press, the electric light bulb to the radio, the telephone to the personal computer—have continually influenced how people live and work. Choose *one invention* and tell how it changed people's lives.
- Community service takes many forms. Some people collect money or goods for worthy causes; some people donate money or goods; some give their time and talent to service projects; and some do all of those things. Think about community service that you have participated in, observed, or read about. Choose *one example* of community service that you think really made a difference, and tell your reader about it.
- A hero or heroine is a person who is admired for courage, outstanding achievements, or noble qualities. Think of heroes or heroines you know or have read about. Choose *one* that you especially admire, and tell your reader why that person is a hero or heroine.
- Sayings, or adages, are short statements that express beliefs in a few well-known words. Choose *one* saying and explain what it means, using examples from your reading, observation, or experience. You may choose one from below or any other that you know:

  - Look before you leap.
  - A penny saved is a penny earned.
  - Behind every cloud is a silver lining.
  - No pain, no gain.

- Think carefully about the issue presented in the following excerpt and the assignment below. "I don't know what your destiny will be, but one thing I know: the only ones among you who will be really happy are those who have sought and found how to serve." (Albert Schweitzer) To what extent is happiness linked to service? Is service, as Schweitzer said, a prerequisite for being happy, or is it possible to be happy without being of service to others? Plan and write an essay in which you develop your point of view on this issue. Support your position with reasoning and examples taken from your reading, studies, experience, or observations.

- All of us are faced with choices, many of which are important and lead to significant consequences. For instance, Anne Frank chose to keep a diary; the Founding Fathers of this country chose to separate from Great Britain; and Marie Curie chose to pursue the study of physics and chemistry. You and members of your family have made important choices, too. Drawing on your reading, observations, and experience, select *one* choice; tell why it was important and what it led to.
- One definition of *challenge* is "a task or situation that tests someone's ability." A challenge may take the form of an illness, a repressive situation, an academic pursuit, a physical confrontation, or any number of other circumstances. The way in which a challenge is met reveals a great deal about one's character. Think of challenges you have read about, observed, and experienced. Choose *one*; tell what was revealed about the person's character by the way the challenge was met.
- A turning point is a time at which a decisive change occurs. Tell about a turning point in your own life or in the life of a character from a book or movie.
- Every novel has key scenes that are essential to the story the book tells. Select some key scenes from the novel you read and explain why they were important to the story.
- A novelist usually characterizes people in the story by what they do, what they say, and how other characters respond to them. Select *one* character from the novel you read and tell about those aspects of his or her character.
- Setting is defined as time, place, and atmosphere of a story. Describe how those aspects of the novel you read contributed to the effectiveness of the book.
- Characters are the people or animals in a story. Select some characters from the novel and explain why they were important to the story.

- The theme, or main idea, of a novel is conveyed through the action of the story. Select some incidents from the novel and explain how they express the theme.
- Most novels revolve around a conflict, or problem. In your essay, tell how the conflict or problem is introduced, developed, and resolved.
- Characters in a novel are often developed through their actions—what they do in particular situations. Show how the actions of *one* character in the chosen novel reveal his or her true nature.
- Authors often use symbols, things that suggest or stand for something else. Select some symbols from the chosen novel and explain how the author used them to represent other things or ideas.
- Although novels are works of fiction, they often reveal truths about human nature. Tell about ways in which the chosen novel is like real life.
- A good author constructs a plot so that the end of the novel depends upon what happens earlier in the story. Tell how, in the chosen novel, key scenes lead logically to the end of the novel.
- When writing a novel, an author uses literary techniques such as symbolism, foreshadowing, flashback, and irony. Select some literary techniques used in the chosen novel and tell how they contribute to the story.
- Sometimes a character in a novel reminds readers of a real person. Select *one* character in the chosen novel and describe ways in which that character is like either someone you know or someone you know about (such as a historical figure, an entertainer, an athlete, etc.).

# APPENDIX C
# SAMPLE INSTRUCTIONS AND PROMPT FOR ASSESSMENT

## INSTRUCTIONS FOR WRITING ASSESSMENT

You will be participating in an assessment that will measure your ability to **think and write**. Your paper will be judged on these characteristics:

- Overall thinking and organization (most important);
- Sentence sense (completeness, correctness, and variety);
- Word choice;
- Mechanics (punctuation, spelling, capitalization); and
- Handwriting (cursive is preferred).

You will have thirty minutes to write in response to the assignment below. When your teacher tells you to begin, take a few minutes to plan your paper and then begin writing. If you finish before your teacher tells you to stop, look over your paper to see if there are ways you can make it better. Make any changes you want to make and then turn in your paper when the teacher tells you to.

## PLANNING SPACE

This back of this page is yours to plan what you will write. Use it any way you wish, to scribble, cluster, draw, list, or outline your thoughts before you begin your response.

### ASSIGNMENT

One definition of challenge is "a task or situation that tests someone's ability." A challenge may take the form of an illness, a repressive situation, an academic pursuit, a physical confrontation, or any number of other circumstances. The way in which a challenge is met reveals a great deal about one's character. Think of challenges you have read about, observed, and experienced. Choose *one*; tell what was revealed about the person's character by the way the challenge was met.

# APPENDIX D
# SAMPLE ANSWER SHEET

Name_____Grade_____

English Teacher_____

_____

_____
_____
_____
_____
_____
_____
_____
_____
_____
_____
_____
_____
_____
_____
_____
_____
_____
_____
_____
_____
_____
_____

# APPENDIX D

Page _____

# APPENDIX E
# TABLE FOR RECORDING STUDENTS' PERFORMANCE ON WRITING ASSESSMENT

*Abbreviations used in the table:*

| | | | | | |
|---|---|---|---|---|---|
| R | Rating | WC | Word Choice | S-V | Subject-Verb Agreement |
| Str | Structure | Sl | Excessive Slang | Pron | Pronoun |
| Frag | Fragment | Re | Gross Redundancy | Cap | Capitalization |
| RO | Run-On | Sp | Spelling | Punc | Punctuation |

Use | Usage

*Instructions:* Fill in the Score (1.0 to 4.0) and Ratings (1, 2, 3, 4). For slang or redundancy, put a check mark; those notations refer to the entire paper. For remaining items, write the number of notations for each.

| Student Name | Score | Discourse | Syntax | | | | Lexicon | | | | Conventions | | | | | | | Writing |
|---|---|---|---|---|---|---|---|---|---|---|---|---|---|---|---|---|---|---|
| | | R | R | Str | Frag | RO | R | WC | Sl | Re | R | Sp | S-V | Pron | Cap | Punc | Use | R |
| | | | | | | | | | | | | | | | | | | |
| | | | | | | | | | | | | | | | | | | |
| | | | | | | | | | | | | | | | | | | |
| | | | | | | | | | | | | | | | | | | |
| | | | | | | | | | | | | | | | | | | |
| | | | | | | | | | | | | | | | | | | |
| | | | | | | | | | | | | | | | | | | |
| | | | | | | | | | | | | | | | | | | |
| | | | | | | | | | | | | | | | | | | |
| | | | | | | | | | | | | | | | | | | |
| | | | | | | | | | | | | | | | | | | |
| | | | | | | | | | | | | | | | | | | |
| | | | | | | | | | | | | | | | | | | |
| | | | | | | | | | | | | | | | | | | |
| | | | | | | | | | | | | | | | | | | |

APPENDIX E

| Student Name | Score | Discourse | Syntax | | | Lexicon | | | | | Conventions | | | | | | Writing |
|---|---|---|---|---|---|---|---|---|---|---|---|---|---|---|---|---|---|
| | | R | R | Str | Frag | RO | R | WC | Sl | Re | R | Sp | S-V | Pron | Cap | Punc | Use | R |

# APPENDIX F
# ANALYTIC RUBRIC, QUANTIFIED

Assessor _____ (Divisor)   Author _____   Grade _____ Topic _____

No. Lines ÷ 10 =

| Aspect & Guidelines | Exemplary | Competent | Developing | Emergent | Wt. & Pts. |
|---|---|---|---|---|---|
| **Discourse** (a connected series of utterances; a text; thus, aspects of discourse pertain to the whole piece of writing). **Read descriptors and apply your judgment.** | 4 – This is an exemplary paper. It is thoughtful, substantive, and focused, expressed in a consistent, engaging voice. It has a clear central idea that is logically and fully developed | 3 – This is a competent paper. It is well-focused with a clear central idea that is adequately supported. It is coherent and it has a discernible, if inconsistent, voice. | 2 – This is a paper that demonstrates developing skill. It expresses a central idea that addresses the assignment, but there may be lapses in focus, organization, and/or development that detract from its effectiveness. | 1 – This paper is the work of an emergent writer; an attempt at writing that is unable to focus on a topic and organize support for it OR This paper does not address the assignment. | X 50 |
| **Syntax** (the arrangement of words and phrases to create sentences) <br> Structure (*str.*) <br> Fragment (*frag.*) <br> Run-on (*RO*) <br> ___ ÷ ___ (Divisor) (No. per 10 lines) <br> (Total) <br> **OR Underline words to indicate that judgment overrides notation.** | 4 – It is written in complete, well-formed sentences that vary in length and complexity. (It has no str. & no fragments or run-ons except those used for effect.) | 3 – With few exceptions, sentences are complete, well-formed, and varied in length and complexity. (No more than 1 Str., RO, or Frag. per 10 lines) | 2 – Most sentences are complete, but they may lack variety in length and/or complexity, or some may be ill-formed. (More than 1 but fewer than 3 Str., RO, or Frag. per 10 lines) | 1 – It demonstrates little "sentence sense," with many fragments or run-ons and/or little variety in length and complexity. (3 or more Str., RO, or Frag. per 10 lines) | X 20 |
| **Lexicon** (vocabulary) <br> Word Choice (*wc*) <br> ___ ÷ ___ (Divisor) (No. per 10 lines) <br> (Total) <br> Excessive Slang? Yes No <br> Gross Redundancy? Yes No <br> **OR Underline words to indicate that judgment overrides notation.** | 4 – It employs a felicitous range of vocabulary, with no ill-chosen words and no slang or redundancy except when clearly used for effect. (No wc, Sl. or Re) | 3 – It employs an appropriate range of vocabulary. (No more than 1 wc per 10 lines, no excessive slang or gross redundancy) | 2 – The range of vocabulary is limited and/or word choice is sometimes inadequate. (More than 1 but fewer than 3 wc per 10 lines and/or excessive slang or gross redundancy) | 1 – The range of vocabulary is extremely narrow. (3 or more wc per 10 lines and/or excessive slang or gross redundancy) | X 15 |
| **Conventions** (the usual ways of doing something, in this case, writing English) <br> ___ Spelling <br> ___ Subj.-Verb <br> ___ Pronoun <br> ___ Capitalization <br> ___ Punctuation <br> ___ Usage <br> ___ ÷ ___ (Divisor) (No. per 10 lines) <br> (Total) <br> **No override.** | 4 – It adheres to Standard American English conventions of grammar, usage, spelling, punctuation, and capitalization. (No vs) | 3 – With few exceptions, it adheres to Standard American English conventions. (No more than 2 vs per 10 lines) | 2 – With several lapses, it attempts to use the conventions of Standard American English. (More than 2 but fewer than 7 vs per 10 lines) | 1 – Errors in grammar, usage, spelling, punctuation, and/or capitalization abound. (7 or more vs per 10 lines) | X 10 |
| **Handwriting** - Read descriptors and apply your judgment. | 4 – It is neatly written in cursive handwriting. | 3 – It is legibly written in cursive handwriting. | 2 – It is legibly printed | 1 – It is difficult to read | X 5 |
| | | | | Total Points/ Score | |

## Procedures for Scoring

1. Review the descriptions of the ratings for discourse on the rubric.
2. Read the paper through for the quality of discourse. Try to ignore other aspects of writing. (It may help to read the paper aloud.)
3. On the rubric, circle the number of the rating for discourse.
4. Glance again at the handwriting. Circle the number of the rating. (If any of the letters are connected, the writing is considered to be cursive.)
5. On the rubric, fill in the author's name, grade in school, topic, and your name (assessor).
6. Count the number of lines in the essay, counting only lines that have ½ or more filled with writing. If the paper has a title, count it as a line. Write the number of lines in the blank provided (just below the title of the rubric). Divide by 10. Round to the nearest whole number. Write that number in the blanks labeled *divisor* in the first column after syntax, lexicon, and conventions.
7. Read the essay again, making these notations in the margin as you read:

   *str*  to indicate awkward or incorrect structure of a sentence
   *frag*  to denote a fragment
   *RO*  to denote a run-on
   **NOTE: If you mark *str.*, *frag*, or *RO*, do not mark internal errors.**
   *wc*  to indicate inappropriate or incorrect word choice
   *Sl*  to denote excessive slang (Make only once for the whole paper.)
   *Re*  to denote gross redundancy (Make only once for the whole paper.)
   *Sp*  Misspelled word
   *S-V*  Disagreement between subject and verb
   *Pron*  Pronoun problem
   *Cap*  Capitalization error
   *Punc*  Incorrect punctuation
   *Use*  Any error in usage not covered by other notations

8. Count the instances of each notation except for slang and redundancy. Write the number in the space provided on the rubric. Denote excessive slang or gross redundancy by circling *Yes* to indicate that it appeared in the essay.
9. Add the number of notations for syntax, lexicon, and conventions recording the sums in the boxes provided.
10. For Syntax: Divide the total number of notations by the divisor. **Apply your judgment; if your judgment overrides the numbers, underline words in the rubric that conform to your judgment.** If not, use the guidelines in parentheses on the rubric to arrive at a rating. Circle the number of the rating.
11. For Lexicon: Divide the number of notations for word choice by the divisor. **Apply your judgment; if your judgment overrides the numbers, underline words in the rubric that conform to your judgment.** If not, use the guidelines in parentheses on the rubric to arrive at a rating. (Note that, if the essay contains excessive slang or gross redundancy, the rating must be 1 or 2.) Circle the number of the rating.
12. For Conventions: Divide the number of errors by the divisor. Use the guidelines in parentheses on the rubric to arrive at a rating. Circle the number of the rating. (Note that there is no provision for override for the rating of conventions.)
13. Multiply each rating by the weight designated on the rubric, and write the number of points in the spaces provided.
14. Add the points for a total; divide by 100 to arrive at the score.

# APPENDIX G
# SAMPLE INDIVIDUAL REPORT OF INTERRATER RELIABILITY

**INTERRATER RELIABILITY REPORT: JANET SMITH (A PSEUDONYM) (DATE OF STUDY)**

Janet Smith (a pseudonym) scored three papers for this study using the Analytic Rubric, Quantified. The papers were written by tenth-grade students, who wrote about how one person can rekindle the light of another.

Correlations of ratings on the individual aspects of writing ranged from 0.33 on lexicon to 1.0 on discourse. The correlation for syntax, conventions, and handwriting was 0.67. Altogether, the three papers offered fifteen decisions (three papers × five decisions per paper). On ten of those, 67 percent, Janet's ratings agreed with the criteria. This degree of correlation is considered substantial.

The table below shows Janet's ratings in comparison with the criteria (gray indicates agreement), and the database displays details for each paper. Note on the database that, on one paper, all of Janet's ratings agreed with the criteria. As the table indicates, two of Janet's ratings that differed from the criteria were higher, and three were lower.

| Aspect of Writing | Janet's Ratings in Comparison to Criteria | | | | | |
| --- | --- | --- | --- | --- | --- | --- |
| | Same | | Higher | | Lower | |
| | No. | % | No. | % | No. | % |
| Discourse | 3/3 | 100 | 0 | 0 | 0 | 0 |
| Syntax | 2/3 | 67 | 0 | 0 | 1/3 | 33 |
| Lexicon | 1/3 | 33 | 2/3 | 67 | 0 | 0 |
| Conventions | 2/3 | 67 | 0 | 0 | 1/3 | 33 |
| Handwriting | 2/3 | 67 | 0 | 0 | 1/3 | 0 |
| Total | 10/15 | 67 | 2/15 | 13 | 3/15 | 20 |

| Janet Smith - 67% (Substantial) | | | | | | | |
| --- | --- | --- | --- | --- | --- | --- | --- |
| No. | Discourse | Syntax | Lexicon | Conventions | Writing | Score | Scorer |
| 51 | 4 | 3 | 3 | 3 | 4 | 3.55 | Criteria |
| 51 | 4 | 3 | 3 | 3 | 4 | 3.55 | Janet |
| 63 | 3 | 3 | 2 | 3 | 4 | 2.90 | Criteria |
| 63 | 3 | 2 | 3 | 2 | 3 | 2.70 | Janet |
| 75 | 2 | 2 | 2 | 3 | 4 | 2.20 | Criteria |
| 75 | 2 | 2 | 3 | 3 | 1 | 2.20 | Janet |

# APPENDIX H

# SAMPLE DATABASE AND PRELIMINARY ANALYSIS FOR STUDY OF INTERRATER RELIABILITY

Note: Names are pseudonyms. Data are taken from a recent study.

| Assessor | | Reliability | | | | | | Ratings Compared to Criteria | | | 100% on Ind. Essays |
|---|---|---|---|---|---|---|---|---|---|---|---|
| First Name | Last Name | Overall | Discourse | Syntax | Lexicon | Conventions | Handwriting | Same | Higher | Lower | |
| Lydia | Adams | 100 | 100 | 100 | 100 | 100 | 100 | 15 | 0 | 0 | 3(51,63,75) |
| Brianna | Bustos | 80 | 100 | 67 | 33 | 100 | 100 | 12 | 1 | 2 | |
| Kerry | Dawson | 73 | 100 | 67 | 33 | 67 | 100 | 11 | 3 | 1 | |
| Sam | Garris | 87 | 67 | 100 | 67 | 100 | 100 | 13 | 0 | 2 | 2(63,75) |
| Doris | Hayes | 93 | 67 | 100 | 100 | 100 | 100 | 14 | 0 | 1 | 2(63,75) |
| Shaquille | Samson | 87 | 100 | 67 | 100 | 67 | 100 | 13 | 0 | 2 | 2(51,75) |
| | | | | | | | Total | 78 | 4 | 8 | |

Six assessors X 15 decisions each = 90 decisions (or ratings)

Number and percent of ratings the same as criteria: 78, or 87% (This is also the measure of overall reliability for the group.)

Number and percent of ratings higher than criteria: 4, 4%

Number and percent of ratings lower than criteria: 8, 9%

Number and percent of assessors who attained excellent overall reliability: 5, or 83%

Number and percent of assessors who attained substantial overall reliability: 1, or 17%

Number and percent of assessors who attained excellent reliability in discourse: 4, 67%

Number and percent of assessors who attained excellent reliability in syntax: 3, 50%

Number and percent of assessors who attained excellent reliability in lexicon: 3, 50%

Number and percent of assessors who attained excellent reliability in conventions: 4, 67%

Number and percent of assessors who attained excellent reliability in handwriting: 6, 100%

Names of assessors who attained perfect correlation on individual essay(s): Lydia Adams on 51, 63, and 75; Sam Garris and Doris Hayes on 63 and 75; and Shaquille Samson on 51 and 75

Names of assessors who attained perfect correlation on Discourse: Lydia Adams, Brianna Bustos, Sam Garris, Doris Hayes, Shaquille Samson.

# RESOURCES

- *Designing Writing Tasks for the Assessment of Writing* by Leo Ruth and Sandra Murphy is invaluable as a primer on writing assessment. In a review of the book (posted online), Karen L. Greenberg, director of the National Testing Network in Writing and associate professor of English at Hunter College, CUNY, wrote, *"Designing Writing Tasks* makes a critically important contribution to our understanding of what writing is and of how we should go about assessing it." Published in 1988, it remains a seminal work on the subject.
- The April 2014 issue of *Educational Leadership* (available from ascd. org) has as its theme "Writing: A Core Skill." Although it doesn't specifically target the assessment of writing, it offers a collection of articles that reflect current thinking about the place of writing in the curriculum and effective ways to teach.
- *The Journal of Writing Assessment* (online at journalofwritingassessment.org) offers timely thinking and research on the subject of writing assessment as well as book reviews and a reading list "for reviews of relevant writing assessment publications."
- *Assessing Writing* is an international journal that provides a forum for ideas, research, and practice on the assessment of written language. Find more about it at journals.elsevier.com.

- The *National Council of Teachers of English Standards for the Assessment of Reading and Writing* are available online from ncte.org.
- The American Evaluation Association's *Guiding Principles for Evaluators* are available online from eval.org.

# REFERENCES

American Evaluation Association. *Guiding Principles for Evaluators*. eval.org.

Birnie, Billie. 2015. *A Teacher's Guide to Organizational Strategies for Thinking and Writing*. Lanham, MD: Rowman & Littlefield.

Gallagher, Kelly. 2011. *Write Like This: Teaching Real-World Writing Through Modeling and Mentor Texts*. Portland, ME: Stenhouse.

Patton, Michael Quinn. 1997. *Utilization-Focused Evaluation*. Thousand Oaks, CA: Sage.

National Council of Teachers of English. *Standards for the Assessment of Reading and Writing*. ncte.org.

Strunk Jr., William, and White, E. B. 2005. *The Elements of Style*. New York: The Penguin Press.

Tufte, Virginia. 2006. *Artful Sentences: Syntax as Style*. Cheshire, CT: Graphics Press LLC.

# ABOUT THE AUTHOR

**Billie Birnie** has been teaching writing for most of her life, first to students in elementary, middle, and senior high schools, and in recent years to prospective and experienced teachers.

She also has years of experience in assessing writing—in classrooms, schools, and districts.

Her published writing ranges from poetry and memoir to professional articles and books on teaching and learning. A charter staff member of the Glazer-Lorton Writing Institute in Miami, Florida, Dr. Birnie has received numerous awards for her work in education. She was named Teacher of the Year in two large urban high schools, Distinguished Alumnus by the University of Miami School of Education, and Educator of the Year by Florida International University.